31

DAYS OF
PRAYER
DURING
infertility

Publishing and Design Services | MelindaMartin.me

31

DAYS OF PRAYER DURING

infertility

Lisa Newton

CONTENTS

INTRODUCTION 1

DAY 1: PRAY FOR CLARITY 3

DAY 2: PRAY FOR COMFORT 7

DAY 3: PRAY FOR COMMUNITY 11

DAY 4: PRAY FOR CONFIDENCE 15

DAY 5: PRAY FOR CONTENTMENT 19

DAY 6: PRAY FOR COURAGE 23

DAY 7: PRAY FOR DISCERNMENT 27

DAY 8: PRAY FOR ENDURANCE 31

DAY 9: PRAY FOR FAITH 35

DAY 10: PRAY FOR FREEDOM FROM FEAR 39

DAY 11: PRAY FOR FREEDOM FROM ENVY & JEALOUSY 43

DAY 12: PRAY FOR YOUR FUTURE CHILDREN 47

DAY 13: PRAY FOR GOD'S GLORY 51

DAY 14: PRAY FOR GRACE 55

DAY 15: PRAY FOR GRATEFULNESS 59

DAY 16: PRAY FOR HOPE 63

DAY 17: PRAY FOR INTEGRITY 67

DAY 18: PRAY FOR JOY 71

DAY 19: PRAY FOR MERCY 75

DAY 20: PRAY TO OBEY 79

DAY 21: PRAY FOR OTHERS 83

DAY 22: PRAY FOR PATIENCE 87

DAY 23: PRAY FOR PEACE 91

DAY 24: PRAY FOR STRENGTH 95

DAY 25: PRAY FOR SUFFICIENT FINANCES 99

DAY 26: PRAY FOR TRUE BELIEF 103

DAY 27: PRAY FOR TRUST 107

DAY 28: PRAY FOR WISDOM 111

DAY 29: PRAY FOR WISE DECISIONS 115

DAY 30: PRAY FOR YOUR MARRIAGE 119

DAY 31: PRAY FOR YOUR SPECIFIC SITUATION 123

ABOUT THE AUTHOR 127

To my husband, Tom, who has taught me much about prayer, and who has so lovingly and patiently dealt with my own struggle to pray aloud. I'm so glad I'm walking through this journey of infertility with you by my side. I love you more.

To all my blog readers who have been praying for me—thank you. Your empathy, understanding, and friendship help to ease the burden of infertility. I'm so privileged and humbled to share this journey with you.

"Now all glory to God, who is able, through his mighty power at work within us, to accomplish infinitely more than we might ask or think. Glory to him in the church and in Christ Jesus through all generations forever and ever! Amen."

—Ephesians 3:20-21

I wrote this book because I'm terrible at prayer. I'm really insecure about praying aloud, even when it's just me and my husband. I often fall asleep when I pray silently at night or early in the morning. Deep, authentic prayer has always been a struggle for me.

Actually, I didn't start off with the intention to write a book. I heard about the 31 Day blogging challenge and I decided I wanted to participate. I'd heard that if you really want to learn about something, then you should write about it. I've been thinking about trying to improve my prayer life for awhile, so I decided it was the perfect time to dive in and figure things out. Several readers encouraged me to turn the blog posts into a book, so that's what I did!

Writing this book didn't make me an expert on prayer. My prayer life hasn't been miraculously changed. But... it's slowly getting better, one tiny step at a time. One of my struggles with prayer was that I felt like I was praying for the same thing over and over again. But now I feel like I have a list of different things to talk to God about. That alone has made this project worth it for me.

Use this book in whatever way works for you. You can choose to work through it one day at a time, or you can skip to the chapters that resonate most with you. It's up to you. The important part is not what you do with these pages. The important thing is that you PRAY.

My hope is that this book encourages you wherever you are in your journey of faith, infertility, and prayer. I hope it helps you connect with God and get to know Him in a deeper way.

.

*"Your own ears will hear him. Right behind you a voice will say,
"This is the way you should go," whether to the right or to the left."*

—Isaiah 30:21

Infertility is full of decisions. You have to decide...

    ...when to see a doctor

    ...which doctor to see

    ...which medicines to take

    ...which treatments you're comfortable with

    ...when to stop treatment

    ...when to try one more time

    ...when to tell people you're trying

    ...who to tell you're trying

It can all get a little confusing and there may not always be a clear choice.

So how do you know what you should do?

The Bible, especially the Psalms, is full of God's people asking for clarity and guidance.

Show me the right path, O Lord; point out the road for me to follow. Lead me by your truth and teach me, for you are the God who saves me. All day long I put my hope in you.

—Psalm 25:4-5

Let me hear of your unfailing love each morning, for I am trusting you. Show me where to walk, for I give myself to you.

—Psalm 143:8

Teach me to do your will, for you are my God. May your gracious Spirit lead me forward on a firm footing.

—Psalm 143:10

Scripture instructs us to turn to God and His Word when we need guidance on what to do. **When we rely on His knowledge instead of our own understanding, He will guide us.**

*Trust in the Lord with all your heart;
do not depend on your own understanding.
Seek his will in all you do, and he will show
you which path to take.*

—Proverbs 3:5-6

As you pray today, ask God to guide you and give you clarity when you make decision on your infertility journey.

For further reflection...

What do you need guidance or clarity for right now?

_____

Read the following verses from Psalm 119.

- What do God's words give us? (verse 30)

- How valuable are God's instructions to us? (verse 72)

- What lights our way as we walk down our path? (verse 105)

Write out a prayer below asking God to give you clarity in your fertility decisions.

_____

_____

_____

_____

_____

To access bonus materials & chapter resources, please go to

http://www.amateurnester.com/31DaysResources

The Lord will comfort Israel again and have pity on her ruins. Her desert will blossom like Eden, her barren wilderness like the garden of the Lord. Joy and gladness will be found there. Songs of thanksgiving will fill the air.

—Isaiah 51:3

Apparently my cat, Hemingway, is quite the fighter. He was acting lethargic a few days ago so I took him to the vet. An examination (and a partial head shave!) revealed multiple puncture wounds and scratches on his head and in his ear. I was horrified when I realized how much pain he was in.

Since then, I've done everything in my power to comfort my cat while he heals. I bought him some new toys. He's been getting extra head rubs. I bought chicken-flavored baby food to mix with his antibiotics. And he spent the last two nights nestled between me and my husband in our bed.

If I am so concerned about comforting my cat, imagine how concerned God is with comforting us, His people, when we are suffering.

The translation above says that the Lord will have *"pity"* on our ruins, but I like the word used in the NIV translation: *compassion.* **God looks with compassion on our ruins.**

Sometimes it feels like infertility leaves me with nothing but ruins: ruined dreams, ruined plans, ruined body, and a ruined bank account. Some of you may have also experienced ruined friendships or ruined marriages due to infertility.

But when we look at the second sentence, we see that God promises restoration. He talks of deserts blossoming and songs of thanksgiving. And the one that captures my attention: ***barren wilderness blossoming.***

Oh, how I long for the day when my literal barrenness will be transformed into something that rivals God's own garden! Maybe a baby will grow from that garden, and maybe not. His promise of restoration doesn't guarantee me a baby. But if He's comparing it to his own personal garden, then whatever it is, **it must be beautiful.**

Until I see that transformation, I am comforted by the fact that God sees my pain. He's orchestrating events and circumstances to help me heal and show me I'm loved. I just need to keep my eyes open to see them.

As you pray today, ask God to help you see His acts of comfort and compassion toward you.

For further reflection...

2 Corinthians 7:6 tells us that God often comforts us through the presence of another person. Who has God used in your life to comfort you?

_____

_____

Visualize the driest, bleakest desert landscape you've ever seen. How do you think you'd feel after spending some time there?

Now think about the most beautiful, lushest garden you've ever seen. How you would feel after moving from the desert you describe above to the garden scene you're picturing?

_____

_____

Read the verses below. Consider writing out each one.

Psalm 71:21

_____

_____

Psalm 119:76

_____

_____

Isaiah 49:13

_____

_____

Isaiah 66:13

_____

_____

Matthew 5:4

_____

_____

Use some of the words and imagery you wrote in the questions above to write out a prayer. Thank God for the comfort you've received in the past and ask for His continued comfort in the days ahead.

_____

_____

_____

_____

_____

To access bonus materials & chapter resources, please go to

http://www.amateurnester.com/31DaysResources

Share each other's burdens, and in this way obey the law of Christ.

—Galatians 6:2

There is one thing I know for certain about infertility: you don't want to go through it alone. But it can feel like a tremendous risk to open yourself up to a connection with someone else going through infertility.

"What if she gets pregnant and I don't?"

"What if my treatments work and hers don't?"

"It's hard enough to go through my own pain. I don't want to get too involved with someone else's."

The Bible tells us to bear one another's burdens. It seems counterintuitive, but when we bear someone else's burdens, our own load is lightened in the process.

God shows up in community (Matthew 18:20). He speaks to us through the lives and words of others. I don't know about you, but I often feel like God provides comfort, encouragement, and wisdom to me through the interactions I have with other infertility-sisters.

We need to resist the temptation to withdraw and isolate ourselves during infertility. We may think it would be easier to do this alone. We wouldn't have to deal with the awkward comments and questions. We'd have a lot more privacy.

But we'd be missing out on so much love and prayer sent our way. Yes, Jesus often withdrew to be alone, but he also spent a lot of his time traveling with, eating with, living with, and just being with eleven other men. His entire ministry took place in the context of community.

If we are to become more like Christ, we must embrace the idea of community.

Just the fact that you're reading this means that you are open to the idea of gaining wisdom from someone else's infertility experience. Let me encourage you (and myself– I'm preaching to myself here!) to take it deeper and connect with people who are willing to bear your burdens and let you bear theirs.

As you pray today, ask God to connect you to a community of people committed to sharing each other's burdens during infertility.

For further reflection...

Have you tended to withdraw and isolate or seek community since your infertility struggle began?

_____

Why do you think that is?

_____

What are some ways you can actively seek out community? If you're already involved in a community, how can you reach out and welcome new members?

_____

Read the following verses. Consider writing each one out.

Romans 15:7

_____

_____

Hebrews 10:24-25

_____

_____

1 Thessalonians 5:14

_____

_____

Write out a prayer below asking God to connect you with the right community and to connect you with other burden-bearers.

_____

_____

_____

_____

_____

_____

To access bonus materials & chapter resources, please go to

http://www.amateurnester.com/31DaysResources

*But blessed are those who trust in the Lord and
have made the Lord their hope and confidence.*

—Jeremiah 17:7

The longer I walk this road through infertility, the more I understand that Christ is the only thing in which I can have full confidence.

When we first started trying to conceive, I put my confidence in my cycle charts. I faithfully tracked my daily temperatures and fertility symptoms, knowing that I'd certainly be pregnant in a few months.

When fertility testing revealed less-than-stellar sperm and a luteal phase defect, I put my confidence in Clomid and the IUIs. Surely they would correct our problems and we would conceive soon.

After three negative IUIs, we put our hopes in IVF. Two failed fresh cycles and one failed frozen cycle later, my confidence in assisted reproductive technology is shattered.

We have plans to continue trying IVF in the next few months. **But I'm no longer confident that technology will help us conceive a child.**

What I am confident in is this: **If God's plan is for me to give birth to a child, then He (and He alone) will make it happen.** Maybe it will be through IVF, or maybe I'll have a miracle natural pregnancy.

If God's plan for me doesn't include pregnancy, then I'm confident He has something else up His sleeve.

I'll admit I'm terrified of what His plan might be. But if I really believe God is who I say He is (loving, good, all-powerful), then I must be confident that His plan is wonderful and perfect.

As you pray today, ask God to give you confidence in His goodness, His love, and His plan for you.

For further reflection...

Have you been tempted to put your confidence in other things besides God during your infertility journey?

_____

Write out your definition of the word "confidence."

_____

_____

Read the following verses. Consider writing each one out.

Psalm 71:5

_____

_____

Hebrews 4:16

_____

_____

Hebrews 13:6

_____

_____

1 John 5:14

_____

_____

Using some of the words you wrote for your definition of confidence, write out a prayer to God confirming your confidence in His plan for you. If you can't fully embrace that confidence yet, write out a prayer asking Him to give you full and complete confidence in Him.

_____

_____

_____

_____

_____

_____

To access bonus materials & chapter resources, please go to

http://www.amateurnester.com/31DaysResources

So if we have enough food and clothing, let us be content.

—1 Timothy 6:8

Contentment during infertility is something I'm still learning more about and struggling. For me, it goes beyond discontentment with being childless. It heads down that slippery slope of getting caught up in the lie that I'd be more content if I had nicer things in the middle of infertility. As I tried to type today's post, I realized that if I tried to share advice or wisdom on this topic, it would be cliche at best and lies at worst. So I've decided to let wiser men and women do most of the heavy lifting today. Here are some insights that I hope will be helpful and encouraging to you.

*Not that I was ever in need, for I have learned
how to be content with whatever I have.*

—*Philippians 4:11*

The Reformation Study Bible points out that Paul isn't denying the fact that he often lacks something. Rather, he "[testifies] that he is content to live both in plenty and in want." His contentment is not based on his material possessions.

Maltbie D. Babcock, a 19th century preacher, elaborates further on the idea that contentment doesn't depend on what we're lacking. It has everything to do with how we view what we do have.

"Contentment is not satisfaction. It is the grateful, faithful, fruitful use of what we have, little or much. It is to take the cup of Providence, and call upon the name of the Lord. What the cup contains is its contents. To get all that is in the cup is the act and art of contentment. Not to

drink because one have but half a cup, or because one does not like its flavour, or because somebody else has silver to one's own glass, is to lose the contents; and that is the penalty, if not the meaning, of discontent. No one is discontented who employs and enjoys to the utmost what he has. It is high philosophy to say, we can have just what we like if we like what we have; but this much at least can be done, and this is contentment: to have the most and best in life by making the most and best of what we have."

G.K. Chesterton would have agreed:

"True contentment is a real, even an active virtue – not only affirmative but creative. It is the power of getting out of any situation all there is in it."

As you pray today, ask God to help you be content in your circumstances—especially when it comes to finances and material things during infertility. Pray that you wouldn't look to what you own to make you content.

For further reflection...

Read Ecclesiastes 1:8 below. Do you ever find yourself feeling the discontentedness the writer describes? Explain.

_____

_____

Everything is wearisome beyond description. No matter how much we see, we are never satisfied. No matter how much we hear, we are not content.

One of the antidotes to discontentment is gratitude. Henri Nouwen wrote:

> *"Resentment and gratitude cannot coexist, since resentment blocks the perception and experience of life as a gift. My resentment tells me that I don't receive what I deserve. It always manifests itself in envy."*

As an exercise in gratitude, list some of the material blessings you've received.

_____

_____

Read each of the following verses. Consider writing out each one.

1 Timothy 6:6-8

_____

_____

Philippians 4:11-13

_____

_____

Matthew 6:31-33

_____

_____

Write out a prayer below asking God to help you be content in your circum-stances—especially when it comes to finances and material things during infertility. Pray that you wouldn't look to what you own to make you content.

_____

_____

_____

_____

_____

_____

To access bonus materials & chapter resources, please go to

http://www.amateurnester.com/31DaysResources

DAY 6: PRAY FOR COURAGE

So be strong and courageous,
all you who put your hope in the Lord!

—Psalm 31:24

My life is a little like the TV show "Friday Night Lights" in that my husband is head coach of a high school varsity football team. We only watched a few episodes of the show on Netflix before we had to stop watching because it hit a little too close to home!

Last night was the sixth football game of the season. I usually sit in the stands with my parents or friends. But my parents couldn't make it to the game, and the friends that came told my husband they were going to bring along some of their friends. One of the women is six months pregnant.

Even on the best night, football games make me extremely anxious. The outcome of the game greatly influences my husband's mood for the coming week. I don't like crowds and loud noises, but football games, by nature, are crowded and noisy! Throw in a lack of parking, freezing weather, and people screaming insults at my husband and I'm a nervous wreck!

So when I found out I was supposed to sit with a pregnant woman, I envisioned fighting back tears the entire game, trying not to look at her swollen belly. I decided I couldn't add another stressor to the evening. I let fear get the best of me, and I asked my husband to text our friends and tell them I wouldn't be able to sit with them.

Luckily, our friends are gracious and understanding, but now I'm embarrassed by my lack of courage. I'm so afraid of making a scene or feeling sad that I miss out on opportunities to connect with people.

I've been avoiding pregnant women for nearly three years now. While it's a healthy form of self-care for me to opt-out of baby-centered events like showers or dedications, I'm realizing that I need to be braver when it comes to interacting with pregnant women at other types of events.

I need to pray for courage. Do you, too?

Maybe you're afraid to make that first appointment with the fertility specialist.

Maybe you feel led to share your story with someone, but haven't yet had the courage.

Maybe you know deep down that it's time to stop treatment, but you're scared to face the feelings that will bring.

Joshua 1:9 tells us to be strong and courageous because God will be with us no matter what. And Psalm 34:4 seems to suggest that praying is one way to alleviate fear.

As you pray today, ask God to give you courage when your infertility causes you fear. Ask Him to help you remember that is He always with you.

For further reflection...

Where do you need more courage in your infertility journey?

_____

Read Joshua 1:9 and Matthew 14:27. What reason do those verses give for not being afraid?

_____

Read each verse. Consider writing out each one.

Psalm 34:4

_____

_____

Psalm 46:1-3

_____

_____

Psalm 112:1-8

_____

_____

Proverbs 3:21-26

_____

_____

Proverbs 31:25

_____

_____

Write out a prayer asking God to give you courage in your specific situation.

_____

_____

_____

_____

_____

_____

To access bonus materials & chapter resources, please go to

http://www.amateurnester.com/31DaysResources

Dear friends, do not believe everyone who claims to speak by the Spirit. You must test them to see if the spirit they have comes from God. For there are many false prophets in the world.

—1 John 4:1

I've been in church and in Christian circles my whole life, but I've never had anyone prophesy over me until I went public about our infertility.

These "prophecies" usually come in different forms. We had several people say we were going to have a baby "very soon." How soon is soon? Beats me! During my first IVF, one acquaintance said she had a dream from God that we'd get pregnant with that cycle. We did, but it was a chemical pregnancy. Does that count as a fulfilled prophecy?

I do believe that God gives people insight into future events through other people or dreams. There certainly are many Biblical examples of that happening, and I know that many of my infertility-sisters have experienced prophecies being spoken over them. But I admit I've personally been very uncomfortable with the idea of it happening to me, because I also know that there are false prophecies.

How do we discern if a message or word from someone else is truly from God?

I've been attending a weekly Bible study* and the lesson this week was about how to identify a true prophecy. I found it to be tremendously helpful. Here's what I learned:

Since prophecies happen outside of Scripture, they are always incomplete. (1 Corinthians 13:9)

In other words, if someone claims to have a step-by-step vision or a complete and total picture of what's going to happen, it is not legitimate. Prophecies always leave room for the mystery of God.

All prophecies must stand up to the test of Scripture. (Acts 17:11, Matthew 7:15)

If a prophecy goes against anything written in Scripture, it cannot be from God. The vision and its messenger must acknowledge Christ's deity. So if someone claims they know all the details about how you'll build your family, but they don't believe Jesus is who Scripture says He is– then the prophecy is not legitimate.

Consider the Messenger

If the message or prophecy passes the two tests, we need to consider the person who spoke it. Do they show evidence of Christ in their life? Obviously, no one is perfect, but to the best of your knowledge are they seeking to grow in their relationship with Christ?

Finally, PRAY about the message you've received.

Ask God to help you discern whether or not it was truly from Him.

As you pray today, ask God to help you discern whether the messages, words, or prophecies you've received (or will receive) from others are truly from him.

Note: I am not a theologian. I don't claim to understand all the doctrines of prophecy or know exactly how discernment works. I believe there is always going to be an aspect of mystery to God. We cannot fully understand how God works or what His plans are. I merely seek to share some of the teaching I've been blessed to receive recently, and to encourage you to view prophecies with a critical eye. Do not let this devotional be the only thing you know about prophecy. I highly encourage you to study this on your own, pray about it, and talk to your pastor!

DAY 7: PRAY FOR DISCERNMENT

For further reflection...

Have you ever received a word, a message, or a vision from someone else who claimed it was from God? If so, describe it below.

_____

_____

What are two criteria for legitimate prophecies? (See Acts 17:11 and 1 Corinthians 13:9).

1. _____

2. _____

Read the verses below. Consider writing out each one.

I found it useful to study the following verses in the ESV translation. It's available for free on BibleGateway.com

Acts 2:16-21

_____

_____

1 Corinthians 14:3

_____

_____

Philippians 1:9-10

_____

_____

Hebrews 5:14

_____

_____

Write out a prayer below asking God to help you discern whether people's predictions and prophecies are truly from Him.

_____

_____

_____

_____

_____

_____

To access bonus materials & chapter resources, please go to

http://www.amateurnester.com/31DaysResources

We also pray that you will be strengthened with all his glorious power so you will have all the endurance and patience you need...

—Colossians 1:11

I often talk say that infertility is a journey. It's been almost three years for me. Others have traveled this road for much longer, while some are just starting out.

No matter how long your journey is, there will be days when it seems too much. That's when we need to rely on Christ's power to get us through.

But endurance is more than just getting through without giving up.

The word we translate as *endurance* in the verse above comes from the Greek word *hypomonēn*. According to Thayer's Greek Lexicon, this word is used several times in the Bible to describe the "characteristic of a [person] who's unswerved from [their] deliberate purpose and [their] loyalty to faith and piety by even the greatest trials and sufferings."

Unswerved from our deliberate purpose and our loyalty to faith. That's more than just getting through!

I don't merely want to survive infertility. I want to be unswerved and steadfast! Don't you?

As you pray today, ask God to help you remain unswerved in your purpose and in your loyalty to him during your sufferings.

For further reflection...

Colossians 1:11 uses the Greek word *hypomonēn* to describe the "characteristic of a [person] who's unswerved from [their] deliberate purpose and [their] loyalty to faith and piety by even the greatest trials and sufferings." How does this definition change your understanding of the word "endurance?"

_____

_____

What would it look like for you to be *unswerved* in your purpose and your loyalty to your faith?

_____

_____

Read the verses below. Consider writing out each one.

Romans 5:3, 15:4

_____

_____

2 Corinthians 6:4

_____

_____

Hebrews 10:36

_____

_____

James 1:3, 5:11

_____

_____

Write out a prayer asking God for endurance.

_____

_____

_____

_____

_____

To access bonus materials & chapter resources, please go to

http://www.amateurnester.com/31DaysResources

The apostles said to the Lord, "Show us how to increase our faith".

—Luke 17:5

I don't know about you, but I have never heard anyone say, "I have enough faith. I don't need anymore."

We can always use more faith—especially when it comes to our infertility journeys.

The dictionary defines faith as "complete trust or confidence in someone or something," and Hebrews 11:1 says it's the "confidence that what we hope for will actually happen [and] assurance about things we cannot see."

More trust? More confidence? More assurance?

Yes, please!

So how do we increase our faith?

Romans 10:17 gives us simple instructions: Faith comes from hearing the Word of Christ. In other words, faith comes through Scripture.

The more we hear, read, and meditate on Christ's words (Scripture), the more our faith will increase.

This doesn't mean we need to spend six hours a day reading our Bible. We should however, make an effort to be hearing and reading God's Word on a regular basis.

I sometimes have trouble reading my Bible consistently, so I have to get creative. I've really enjoyed listening to the audio version of certain translations available on the Bible Gateway app and website*. I also love listening to sermons and Scripture meditation podcasts like *Pray as You Go* and *The Daily Disconnect*.

As you pray for increased faith today, ask God to give you a love and hunger for His Word.

For further reflection...

Write out the definition of faith found in Hebrews 11:1.

_____

_____

Romans 10:17 says that faith comes through hearing the Word. Are you regularly hearing or reading Scripture? If not, list one way you can incorporate more Scripture into your life.

_____

Read the verses below. Consider writing each one out.

Matthew 9:21-22

_____

_____

Matthew 21:21

_____

_____

2 Corinthians 5:7

_____

_____

Ephesians 3:12

_____

_____

Ephesians 6:16

_____

_____

1 Peter 1:7

_____

_____

2 Peter 2:5-6

_____

_____

Write out a prayer asking God to increase your faith and give you a hunger for His Word.

_____

_____

_____

_____

_____

To access bonus materials & chapter resources, please go to

http://www.amateurnester.com/31DaysResources

I prayed to the Lord, and he answered me.
He freed me from all my fears.

—Psalm 34:4

Nearly every book in the Bible has a verse that tells us not to fear. In fact, *Fear not!* is the most common command in Scripture. (Or, as one pastor has said, it's the most loving invitation).

But infertility is scary. We're facing the loss of our dreams, our health, and our bank account. Don't we have every reason to be afraid?

When we're tempted to give into fear, let's meditate instead on several promises.

- God is our helper. We have no reason to fear anything other humans can do to us (Hebrews 13:6).

- God is always with us and will strengthen us when we need it (Isaiah 41:10).

- God upholds us (Isaiah 41:13).

- God walks with us and comforts us during scary times (Psalm 23:4).

- He gives us peace instead of fear (John 14:27).

Which one of these promises most resonates with you? I tend to fear the journey more than the destination, so His promise of strength is the most precious to me.

As you pray today, ask God to deliver you from your fear. Pick the promises that resonates most with you and thank God for that specific promise.

For further reflection...

What about infertility scares you the most?

_____

_____

_____

Look up each of the following verses and write down the promise you see in it.

Joshua 1:9

_____

_____

Psalm 118:6

_____

_____

Proverbs 3:24

_____

_____

Jeremiah 1:8

_____

_____

John 14:27

_____

_____

Using an online Bible concordance (such as BibleGateway.com), search for "Do not be afraid," or "Fear not." Read through some of the many instances of this phrase. Consider writing out some or all of the verses.

_____

_____

_____

_____

Write out a prayer to God asking him to deliver you from fear.

_____

_____

_____

_____

_____

_____

_____

To access bonus materials & chapter resources, please go to

http://www.amateurnester.com/31DaysResources

DAY 11: PRAY FOR FREEDOM FROM ENVY & JEALOUSY

Envy and jealousy will kill a stupid fool.

—Job 5:2

For me, it strikes most often at Target and the grocery store. Baby-envy. If you've wrestled with infertility for any amount of time you'll know exactly what I'm talking about.

I find that it comes in two forms. The first comes when I see women who I consider to be "unworthy" of motherhood:

The girl who can't be older than 15 pushing a stroller with one hand and patting her pregnant belly with the other.

The mom who screams at her toddler to stop crying after she trips and falls.

The second form comes when I see someone who appears to have the life I want:

The gorgeous woman who calmly walks the store aisles, sipping Starbucks while her peaceful baby sleeps quietly.

The couple walking hand-in-hand down the baby aisle, aiming the gift registry guns at cute little outfits.

At best, it will put you in a bad mood. At worst, it can destroy relationships and leave you with a wounded soul.

Whenever I sense these feelings of jealousy and envy swelling up inside me, I have to make a choice. I can give into them and ruminate on them, throwing myself a major pity party.

Or, I can acknowledge my sadness surrounding my own circumstances, thank God for the lives of the families I encounter, and pray against being consumed by jealousy and envy.

Sometimes I can do this in a few seconds or minutes. Sometimes it takes much longer. But it won't happen naturally. I must *choose* to fight my jealousy with prayer.

During your prayer time today, ask the Lord to help you resist the temptation to wallow in jealousy and envy.

For further reflection...

When do you most often find yourself struggling with envy and/or jealousy?

_____

_____

Describe a circumstance in which you have seen the negative effects of jealousy or envy.

_____

_____

Read each verse below. Consider writing each one out.

Proverbs 14:30

_____

_____

Proverbs 27:4

_____

_____

Song of Solomon 8:6

_____

_____

1 Corinthians 13:4

_____

_____

James 3:14-15

_____

_____

Write a prayer asking God to help you love the people you're jealous of and to resist the temptation to wallow in jealousy.

_____

_____

_____

_____

_____

_____

To access bonus materials & chapter resources, please go to

http://www.amateurnester.com/31DaysResources

For I will pour out water to quench your thirst and to irrigate your parched fields. And I will pour out my Spirit on your descendants, and my blessing on your children.

—Isaiah 44:3

Praying for our future children can be a tremendous act of faith and trust in God. It's something we can do regardless of whether children come to us through pregnancy, surrogacy, or adoption.

Many of us have boxes, closets, or rooms full of baby items we've collected in anticipation of giving them to our children one day. I like to think that our prayers can be another form of gift-giving to our future children.

What can you pray for your future child? Here are some suggestions:

That they would know God.

- Matthew 19:13-15

- 2 Timothy 2:10

That they would love His word.

- Deuteronomy 6:6-7

- Psalm 19:10

- Psalm 119:97

That they would be confident of who they are in Christ.

- Jeremiah 1:5

- 1 Peter 2:9

- 1 John 3:1-2

That they would love and serve others.

- Colossians 3:12

- 1 Tim 6:18-19

As you pray today, ask God to bring to mind other blessings you can be praying over your future children.

For further reflection...

Is it easy or difficult for you to pray things for your future child(ren)? Why?

_____

_____

What's the one thing you want to pray for the most for your future child(ren)?

_____

_____

As you grow more comfortable praying for your future child(ren), what are other things you can pray for them?

_____

_____

Read the following examples of parents praying for their children. Consider writing each verse out.

Genesis 17:18

_____

_____

2 Samuel 12:16

_____

_____

1 Chronicles 29:19

_____

_____

Job 1:5

_____

_____

Write out a prayer below for your future child(ren).

_____

_____

_____

_____

_____

To access bonus materials & chapter resources, please go to

http://www.amateurnester.com/31DaysResources

In the same way, let your good deeds shine out for all to see, so that everyone will praise your heavenly Father.

—Matthew 5:16

I often talk about how sharing your infertility story helps others. No one going through infertility wants anyone else to suffer, but there's comfort in knowing you're not the only one going through this experience.

But sharing your story also serves another purpose: glorifying God.

What exactly does that mean?

It means telling others about who is He, what He's done, and what He will do. It means acknowledging Him as the source of everything good in your life, and as sovereign during the difficult times.

Some of us glorify God in the midst of our infertility by blogging or writing.

Others glorify God in a more private manner, not by sharing their stories on the internet, but in church groups, Bible studies, coffee meetings, family dinners, or lunch dates.

I don't think the point is *how* we glorify God, but *that* we glorify Him. 1 Corinthians 10:31 says "So whether you eat or drink, or whatever you do, do it all for the glory of God."

Do you see that phrase? **Whatever you do**. Allow me the liberty to paraphrase...

So whether you do IVF or IUI... do it all for the glory of God.

So whether you blog or share you story with just one friend... do it all for the glory of God.

So whether you adopt or live a childless life... do it all for the glory of God.

So whether you pursue treatment or pray for a miracle... do it all for the glory of God.

Infertility is a dark place. So many of our infertility sisters are stuck in places of hopelessness and despair. It's not wrong to experience these emotions, but God does not want us to stay there indefinitely. If you and I have even the slightest amount of hope, faith, or light we must share it with them and with anyone who knows about our journey.

Here's another way to put it: You're here to be light, bringing out the God-colors in the world. God is not a secret to be kept. We're going public with this, as public as a city on a hill. If I make you light-bearers, you don't think I'm going to hide you under a bucket, do you? I'm putting you on a light stand. Now that I've put you there on a hilltop, on a light stand—shine! Keep open house; be generous with your lives. By opening up to others, you'll prompt people to open up with God, this generous Father in heaven.

—*Matthew 5:15-16 (MSG)*

Let's shine our lights, ladies.

As you pray today, ask God to help you glorify Him in circumstances and in your decisions.

For further reflection...

Use a dictionary or www.thesaurus.com to look of synonyms of the word *glorify*. Write them below. Circle the synonyms which resonate with you the most.

_____

_____

Using the synonyms as inspiration, jot down some ways in which you might be able to glorify God in the midst of your infertility.

_____

_____

Read each verse below. Consider writing each verse out.

Psalm 86:8-10, 96:1-3, 115:1

_____

_____

Isaiah 42:12

_____

_____

John 1:5

_____

_____

2 Corinthians 2:4-6

_____

_____

1 Peter 2:12

_____

_____

Revelation 4:11

_____

_____

Write out a prayer below in which you glorify God for who He is and what's He's done.

_____

_____

_____

_____

_____

To access bonus materials & chapter resources, please go to

http://www.amateurnester.com/31DaysResources

*May God's grace be eternally upon all
who love our Lord Jesus Christ.*

—Ephesians 6:24

One of the most recognizable songs in the world is "Amazing Grace." Even people who don't identify as Christians know the words and find some comfort in it.

But what is grace?

I looked up definitions in all the major dictionaries, and I like Google's the best:

"[Grace is] the free and unmerited favor of God, as manifested in the salvation of sinners and the bestowal of blessings."

Just the idea of having the favor of God should be enough to blow our minds. He offers us His ultimate grace in the form of salvation. It's free, unconditional, and available to everyone—no matter what we've done or who we are.

We only have to do one thing in order receive it: believe. (See John 3:16 and Ephesians 2:8-9)

His grace doesn't stop at salvation. He gives us new graces every day (Lamentations 3:23). We only need to be willing to receive them.

Extending His grace to others

Another amazing thing about God's grace is that receiving it empowers us to give it away.

Stop for a moment and reflect on that... God often chooses to use us—broken, sinful, messed up people—as vessels of His love for other people.

So, how do we go about extending grace in the middle of infertility?

Think about how many people you've encountered during infertility who do not merit your favor.

The co-worker you barely know who tells you infertility is a sign from God that you'd make a bad parent...

The friend who called you selfish when you gently declined her baby shower invitation (and sent a very nice gift)...

The husband who doesn't see the need to comfort you as you cry over the arrival of your period...

None of these people deserve grace. But that's exactly the definition of grace, isn't it? *Unmerited* favor and blessings.

We shouldn't allow ourselves to be abused, and there are healthy boundaries we sometimes need to put in place to protect ourselves. But we can extend grace by praying for people who hurt us. We can refuse to spread gossip and vitriol. We can love and serve them to the best of our abilities.

God will give us the grace to do so. And that's amazing, indeed!

For further reflection...

Read the quote below and write down what you think the defining characteristic of grace is.

> *"Grace...means that God is pursuing you. That God forgives you. That God sanctifies you. When you are apathetic toward God, He is never apathetic toward you. When you don't desire to pray and talk to God, He never grows tired of talking to you. When you forget to read your Bible and listen to God, He is always listening to you. Grace means that your spirituality is upheld by God's stubborn enjoyment of you."*
>
> *—from "Charis: God's Scandalous Grace for Us" by Preston Sprinkel*

What kinds of graces have you received from God during your season of infertility?

_____

_____

Who is one person you can extend grace to? How?

_____

_____

Read the verses below. Consider writing each one out.

Romans 5:16-18, 11:5-6

_____

_____

Ephesians 1:6-8

_____

_____

Hebrews 4:15-16

_____

_____

2 Thessalonians 1:11-12

_____

_____

Write out a prayer below thanking God for the grace you've received and asking him to help you be gracious towards others.

_____

_____

_____

_____

_____

To access bonus materials & chapter resources, please go to

http://www.amateurnester.com/31DaysResources

DAY 15: PRAY FOR GRATEFULNESS

Always be joyful. Never stop praying.
Be thankful in all circumstances, for this is God's will
for you who belong to Christ Jesus.

—1 Thessalonians 5:16-18

I doubt that any of us have rejoiced over the fact that we're struggling with infertility. I don't know about you, but I'm not sending a thank-you card to God for my infertility anytime soon.

BUT... There are so many things I'm grateful for in the midst of my infertility, and I have been able to genuinely thank Him for these things.

The first thing that comes to mind is how infertility has strengthened my marriage. I'm also profoundly grateful for the online infertility community and the wonderful relationships I have with my readers and other bloggers.

But what if infertility has hurt our marriage? Or if we haven't experienced community with others?

Here are a few examples of things for which we can be grateful in any circumstance:

- God's goodness & mercy

- God's promises of strength, comfort, courage, and endurance

- The faith of others (which inspires us)

- The nearness of God

- Our eternal hope and salvation

And even on the bleakest of days, we can be grateful for Christ's victory over death. **Even in death, God is at work on behalf of His people.**

As you pray today, thank God for the good that has come out of your infertility. If you have trouble naming the good, thank Him for the the blessings we have in any circumstance (listed above).

For further reflection...

List some of the good things that have come out of your infertility.

_____

_____

Which of the good things you wrote above has been the most surprising or unexpected?

_____

_____

Read the verses below. Consider writing out each one.

Psalm 107:1, 21-22

_____

_____

Colossians 2:6-8

_____

_____

Colossians 4:2

_____

_____

Romans 8:28

_____

_____

Write out a prayer to God thanking Him for the good that has come from your infertility. Ask Him to help you be thankful even on the days when you have trouble seeing those good things.

_____

_____

_____

_____

_____

_____

To access bonus materials & chapter resources, please go to

http://www.amateurnester.com/31DaysResources

Let all that I am wait quietly before God, for my hope is in him.

—Psalm 62:5

nfertility bloggers like to talk about hope. We say things like "Don't give up hope," or "Put your hope in God."

After years of failed cycles, all this talk about hope can start to sound a little trite. Are we just supposed to keep our fingers crossed and keep wishing for babies?

I think we need to start thinking about hope as something a little deeper, something more substantial.

I love the way M. Esther Lovejoy describes it in her book, *The Sweet Side of Suffering*:

> *"The hope put forth in Scripture is much more in keeping with [a dictionary definition]. It is a claim, an assurance of something not yet realized, but unquestioningly certain. Hope is not crossed fingers, but a settled heart.... [It's] an emotional investment in our future. It is believing that in the end there will be relief or a solution—something that will be better than what we are presently experiencing."*

That's the kind of hope I want. I want to know that even if I never become a parent, God has something better than what I'm going through.

So how do we get hope? Romans 12:12 offers some interesting insight:

> *Rejoice in our confident hope. Be patient in trouble, and keep on praying.*

Rejoice. Be patient. Keep on praying.

As you pray today, ask God to give you hope that He has something better than what we are presently experiencing.

For further reflection...

What kind of sufferings are you currently experiencing?

_____

_____

_____

Look up the verses below. Consider writing out each one.

Psalm 31:24

_____

_____

Psalm 33:20-21

_____

_____

Psalm 119:81, 146-148

_____

_____

Jeremiah 17:7

_____

_____

Romans 12:12, 15:13

_____

_____

Ephesians 1:18

_____

_____

Hebrews 10:23

_____

_____

Write out a prayer asking God to give you hope that He has a plan for us to experiencing something better than our current situation.

_____

_____

_____

_____

_____

_____

To access bonus materials & chapter resources, please go to

http://www.amateurnester.com/31DaysResources

The godly walk with integrity;
blessed are their children who follow them.

—Proverbs 20:7

We live in a town with a large military population. My husband is muscular and bald, so people often mistakenly assume he is in the military. Yesterday we went out for lunch and when the waiter brought the bill he said, "Let me make sure I added your military discount." My husband told him he wasn't in the military, and the waiter left us the check.

A few minutes later, I noticed my husband chuckling to himself. I asked him what was so funny, and he said, "You know, John* wouldn't have corrected the waiter. He would've accepted the discount even though he's not in the military. And he would've made up some elaborate story about when and where we served, and all his deployments." I laughed, too, because I knew he was right about this particular friend. He is famous for making up stories to receive discounts and special treatment. He does not have a reputation for being a man of integrity.

We giggled about our friend's lack of integrity, but the truth is that it's not very funny. The Bible has very strong words about living an integrity-filled life.

The way of the Lord is a stronghold to those with integrity,
but it destroys the wicked.

—Proverbs 10:29

The Lord detests people with crooked hearts,
but he delights in those with integrity.

—Proverbs 11:20

What does it look like to live with integrity in the midst of infertility? Here are a few examples I thought of:

- Being truthful about how much money you spent on healthcare when you do your taxes

- Fundraising for treatment or adoption and actually using the funds for their intended purpose

- Not gossiping about the difficult interactions you have with friends and family who don't understand what infertility is like

- Posting to your infertility blog during your personal time, not when you're at work on company time (This one is SUCH a temptation for me!)

The good news is that integrity reaps many blessings. The two verses above tell us that our integrity "delights" God and that it becomes a "stronghold" (sometimes translated as "protection," or a "safe place") for those who practice it. But my favorite is the promise of a blessing on our children.

Think about that. **One of the best things you can do for your future children is to live an integrity-filled life now!**

As you pray today, ask God to help you live a life of integrity during this season of infertility.

Not his real name.

For further reflection...

Using a thesaurus or thesaurus.com, look up the word *integrity* and write down a few synonyms you find. Circle the ones that resonate the most with you.

_____

_____

Have you ever given thought to how your integrity can challenge and encourage others? Consider the following quote from Chuck Swindoll:

> *"Few things are more infectious than a godly lifestyle. The people you rub shoulders with everyday need that kind of challenge. Not prudish. Not preachy. Just cracker jack clean living. Just honest to goodness, bone-deep, non-hypocritical integrity."*

However, we must be careful not to let our zeal for integrity turn into legalism, or allow ourselves to become wrecked with guilt when we fail. Author and pastor Sam Storms reminds us:

> *"Integrity does not mean sinless,*
> *but it does describe people who by God's grace 'sin less.'"*

Look up the verses below. Consider writing each one out.

2 Samuel 22:26

_____

_____

2 Chronicles 19:7

_____

_____

Job 31:6

_____

_____

Psalm 18:25, 25:21, 26:11, 119:1

_____

_____

Proverbs 2:7

_____

_____

Write out a prayer below asking God to help you live a life of integrity, and to help you remember His grace when you fail.

_____

_____

_____

_____

_____

To access bonus materials & chapter resources, please go to

http://www.amateurnester.com/31DaysResources

Don't be dejected and sad, for the joy of the Lord is your strength.

—Nehemiah 8:10

Stress comes more naturally to us [than joy], and it takes intentional change and obedience to the Spirit to learn to live in joy."

—*Holley Gerth in "You're Going to Be Okay"*

This quote is so true of me. Being joyful requires tremendous effort for me. I've always blamed it on my innate personality, but the truth is that sometimes it's just easier to be stressed out than to be joyful. Sometimes I'm just too tired and too weak to try.

The past few days have been full of struggle and joylessness for me. The burden of a quickly-approaching 3rd IVF cycle is weighing heavily on me. But I've been comforted by a song from my childhood stuck in my head. Perhaps you know it from your Sunday School days, too.

> "The joy of the Lord is my strength (repeat 4x)
> If you want joy you must clap for it (repeat 4x)
> If you want joy you must sing for it (repeat 4x)
> If you want joy you must pray for it" (repeat 4x)

I remember singing this song and switching out the verbs for all kinds of silly actions—jumping, skipping, swaying, running, spinning, etc. As a child, this song was simply a fun way to get the wiggles out. But it planted a profound truth in my heart: **Sometimes joy requires action.**

Perhaps joy will never come naturally, especially in the middle of struggling with infertility. But instead of surrendering to joylessness, **we must fight for**

joy. We must seek after it instead of expecting it to fall in our laps. If we feel we don't have the strength to seek it out, we must remember that strength comes *through* joy, not after it. **In other words, joy provides strength.**

This is hard, I know. Infertility wears us down and messes with our minds. Throw in a little Clomid or Lupron and you've got the makings of crazy. The good news is that joy doesn't just give us strength; it gives us Christ's strength. The weaker we are, the better his strength is perfected in us (2 Cor. 12:9).

So dear friends, I hope you'll join me in fighting for joy throughout all the darkness that infertility can bring.

For further reflection...

Does joy come naturally to you or do you find yourself needing to fight for it?

_____

_____

Read 1 Thessalonians 5:16-18. The NIV Application Commentary says:

> *"[the verse's] emphasis on joy is not so much on the experience of joy, but the active expression of it. Thus the translation "rejoice," which makes it clear that an action or attitude is involved, is preferable to "be joyful," which misleadingly suggests more an emotional state."*

If joy stems more from our expression and action than our emotions, what are some ways you can fight for joy?

_____

_____

Look up the verses below. Consider writing each one out.

Psalm 9:2, 28:7, 34:8, 100:2

_____

_____

Habakkuk 3:17-18

_____

_____

Romans 15:13

_____

_____

2 Corinthians 6:10

_____

_____

Philippians 4:4

_____

_____

Write out a prayer asking God to help you experience His joy even when your emotions don't feel very joyful.

_____

_____

_____

_____

_____

_____

To access bonus materials & chapter resources, please go to

http://www.amateurnester.com/31DaysResources

Listen to my prayer for mercy as I cry out to you for help, as I lift my hands toward your holy sanctuary.

—Psalm 28:2

I did a little bit of studying before writing today's post. One Bible commentary calls Psalm 28 a "Prayer of Distress," and a another Bible dictionary defines *mercy* as "compassion for the miserable."

Distress. Misery.

I know I've felt both of those multiple times during my battle with infertility.

The Psalms is full of prayers for mercy during difficult, miserable times. Many of them were penned by David, who experienced years of persecution from King Saul.

Despite his miserable state, David remained confident in God's mercy. His prayers for mercy are almost always followed by prayers of thanksgiving to God for coming through and actually being merciful.

Praise the Lord! For he has heard my cry for mercy. The Lord is my strength and shield. I trust him with all my heart. He helps me, and my heart is filled with joy. I burst out in songs of thanksgiving. —Psalm 28:6-7

My commentary says that the language used in the original text denotes "not only an earnest desire [for mercy], but an earnest expectation [of mercy]."

As you pray for mercy today, ask God to help you pray with an earnest expectation of the mercy He will give you.

For further reflection...

Why do you think it's so hard to "earnestly expect" God's mercy?

_____

_____

_____

Look up the verses below. Consider writing each one out.

Psalm 6:2, 6:9, 28:6, 40:11, 119:132

_____

_____

Matthew 5:7

_____

_____

Luke 1:49-51

_____

_____

Hebrews 4:16

_____

_____

Write out a prayer asking God for His mercy and for His help in earnestly expecting it.

_____

_____

_____

_____

_____

_____

The lifting of hands has long been viewed as a symbol of asking and receiving from God during prayer. Consider reading your prayer aloud with raised hands.

To access bonus materials & chapter resources, please go to

http://www.amateurnester.com/31DaysResources

78

Restore to me the joy of your salvation,
and make me willing to obey you.

—Psalm 51:12

My parents will tell you I was a pretty obedient child. I remember realizing at a very young age that obeying my parents really was the best thing for me. I understood that the things my parents wanted me to do were for my own good and meant to protect me.

But obedience doesn't seem as black-and-white when you're an adult trying to figure out what it means to obey God in the midst of infertility. It's not like He's given us a list of the Infertility Commandments.

Sometimes we're not sure what He wants us to do.

And we don't always have confidence that what He's asking us to do is in our best interest.

I think this is where prayer comes in. Oswald Chambers gives us this lovely quote:

> *"One great effect of prayer is that it enables the soul to command the body. By obedience I make my body submissive to my soul, but prayer puts my soul in command of my body."*

Even when we're not sure what God is asking us to do, prayer get our souls in the right place to obey when we do hear His voice. Without prayer, it's much more difficult to hear God's voice and instruction.

As you pray today, ask God to help you hear His voice and obey it.

For further reflection...

Read the quote below from missionary Jim Elliot:

> *"Rest in this —it is His business to lead, command, impel, send, call or whatever you want to call it. It is your business to obey, follow, move, respond, or what have you."*

Do you sense God leading, commanding, impelling, sending, or calling you in a certain direction during your infertility journey? Explain below.

_____

_____

Sometimes we're not sure what God is asking of us. Read Matthew 22:36-40 to find out what His greatest commandment is. Write it below.

_____

_____

How can you obey the greatest commandment in the midst of infertility?

_____

_____

Look up the verses below. Consider writing each one out.

Exodus 20:6

_____

_____

Joshua 22:5

_____

_____

Psalm 25:10, 111:10, 119:2Isaiah 26:8

_____

_____

Matthew 5:19, 7:26

_____

_____

Romans 6:16

_____

_____

To access bonus materials & chapter resources, please go to

http://www.amateurnester.com/31DaysResources

82

Confess your sins to each other and pray for each other so that you may be healed. The earnest prayer of a righteous person has great power and produces wonderful results.

—James 5:16

I'm somewhat of a podcast addict. I'll listen to 10-15 podcasts each week. This past week I heard one that has stayed with me for days.

Craig McConnell is one of the bloggers for John Eldredge's *Ransomed Heart* ministry. During one of their recent podcasts, entitled, "The Story You Find Yourself In," he spoke about how he's going through a recurrence of cancer, and how God is teaching him to pray for others even when he's in the middle of deep physical and emotional suffering himself. Around the 11 minute-mark he says:

> *"It feels cruel—when you're suffering—that God would ask you to put your eyes and focus your attention on others...There's no exemptions to love the Lord your God with all your heart, and love others...* **When you suffer you feel justified to be preoccupied with yourself.** *Understandably so. To some degree, necessarily so. And yet in my pain and suffering, God came and said, 'I want you—in your pain and suffering—to love others.' And what felt cruel initially ended up turning into this rich communion with God, where I felt like this must be some of what the cross felt like for Christ. The absolute severe physical and personal pain of the crucifixion, and yet He's concerned for the hearts and lives of others. And his whole heart is turned towards others."*

Did that take your breath away like it did mine? "When you suffer you feel justified to be preoccupied with yourself."

Isn't that so true? I know this has been such a struggle during infertility. My heart is so heavy and so wounded that it's hard sometimes to find room for others and carry their burdens, too.

But our ultimate example is Christ, and when He was in the middle of doing the most difficult thing anyone had ever done (the crucifixion), He prayed for others: "Father, forgive them..." (Luke 23:34).

In our own pain, we can pray for others out of duty, or we can choose to use our prayers as a means of inviting God into our pain even further. It will take tremendous strength to pray during our own time of need, but God will come through and strengthen us in the process.

Pick one or two people to pray for today. Spend some time asking God to give them what they need, and to help you be others-focused even in the midst of your own pain.

DAY 21: PRAY FOR OTHERS

For further reflection...

Do you resonate with Craig McConnell's quote: "When you suffer you feel justified to be preoccupied with yourself"? Why or why not?

_____

_____

Who do you know that needs prayer? List their names and needs below. Choose 2-3 and circle their names.

_____

_____

Look up the verses below. Consider writing each one out.

Job 42:10

_____

_____

Luke 23:32-34

_____

_____

Acts 7:59-60

_____

_____

Philippians 2:3-4

_____

_____

Write out a prayer for the people whose names you circled above.

_____

_____

_____

_____

_____

To access bonus materials & chapter resources, please go to

http://www.amateurnester.com/31DaysResources

This vision is for a future time. It describes the end, and it will be fulfilled. If it seems slow in coming, wait patiently, for it will surely take place. It will not be delayed.

—Habakkuk 2:3

Praying for patience is scary. By definition, patience assumes a wait. So by asking God for patience we're surrendering to the wait.

I don't like waiting. I want what I want—right now!

But Habakkuk 2:3 tells us that God's vision for our life will happen on His timetable.

God is not running late. Everything is going according to (His) schedule. He knows it may feel slow to us, but He promises He's not delayed. He asks us to wait patiently. To trust that He what He has planned for us will actually happen.

As you pray today, ask God to help you wait patiently for His plan to be fulfilled.

For further reflection...

What do you need patience for right now regarding your infertility journey?

_____

_____

What promises do you see regarding His vision in Habakkuk 2:3?

_____

_____

Look up each of the following verses. Consider writing each one out.

Galatians 5:22

_____

_____

Colossians 1:10-12, 3:12-13

_____

_____

James 5:10-11

_____

_____

Write out a prayer below asking God to help you wait patiently for His vision to be fulfilled.

_____

_____

_____

_____

_____

_____

To access bonus materials & chapter resources, please go to

http://www.amateurnester.com/31DaysResources

*Then you will experience God's peace,
which exceeds anything we can understand. His peace will guard
your hearts and minds as you live in Christ Jesus.*

—Philippians 4:7

Think for a moment about all the synonyms for the word *peace*.

Calm.

Stillness.

Tranquility.

Security.

Safety.

Quiet.

Freedom from disturbance.

How many of those words describe your experience with infertility? I'm guessing not many, if any! In fact, our experience can quite often be the exact opposite of peaceful.

In the middle of all the craziness, Scripture shows us how to find peace.

Isaiah 26:3 tells us that our thoughts hold the key to peace.

You will keep in perfect peace all who trust in you, all whose thoughts are fixed on you!

By fixing our thoughts on God, we allow His peace to come on us.

Philippians 4:8-9 also encourages us to seek peace by focusing our thoughts not on the negative, but on the good, pure things we know to be true.

And now, dear brothers and sisters, one final thing. Fix your thoughts on what is true, and honorable, and right, and pure, and lovely, and admirable. Think about things that are excellent and worthy of praise. Keep putting into practice all you learned and received from me—everything you heard from me and saw me doing. Then the God of peace will be with you.

Focusing our thoughts on God is not easy—especially in the middle of difficult circumstances. It's like starting a new workout. Our muscles will ache, we'll be fatigued, and we'll want to take the easy way out by just quitting. But if we stick with the discipline of focusing on what we know to be true about God (He is good, He is loving, He has a plan), our spiritual muscles will gradually get stronger and focusing our thoughts on Him will get easier.

As you pray for peace today, ask God to help you focus your thoughts on Him during difficult times.

For further reflection...

Read 2 Peter 1:2. What does God give us more of as we grow in our knowledge of Him?

_____

_____

Read Psalm 23. List the things this passage says God does for us.

_____

_____

How does the knowledge of what Psalm 23 says God does for us increase your sense of peace?

_____

_____

Look up the verses below. Consider writing each one out.

Romans 5:13

_____

_____

Ephesians 6:14-16

_____

_____

Write out a prayer below asking God to help you know Him more.

_____

_____

_____

_____

_____

_____

To access bonus materials & chapter resources, please go to

http://www.amateurnester.com/31DaysResources

*My health may fail, and my spirit may grow weak, but God remains
the strength of my heart; he is mine forever.*

—Psalm 73:26

My younger brother Peter was a voracious eater as a child. He ate anything you put in front of him (well, except carrots), and never seemed to get full. He'd often get hungry in between meals and ask our mother for a snack, saying, "I need a something to hold me up." His phrase became a part of our family vocabulary and we still say it today.

I don't know about you, but infertility can make me feel real weak. Hormones, emotions, and stress make me cry easier. I get discouraged quicker than I used to. Sometimes I feel broken—both physically and emotionally.

I need something to hold me up.

Isaiah 41:10 says that God will hold us up in His hands during our times of trouble.

Do not be afraid, for I am with you. Don't be discouraged for I am your God. I will   strengthen you and help you. **I will hold you up** *with my victorious right hand.*

This doesn't mean our trouble will disappear. There will still be tough days. But God's strength can sustain us and keep us from utter despair.

As you pray today, ask God to "hold you up" with his strength.

For further reflection...

What do you need strength for right now?

_____

When have you felt God's strength in the past?

_____

Look up the verses below. Consider writing out each one.

Psalm 18:32, 22:19, 28:7, 29:11

_____

_____

Isaiah 41:10

_____

_____

Ephesians 3:16, 6:10

_____

_____

Philippians 4:13

_____

_____

Write out a prayer asking God to remind you of the times He gave you strength before and to help you trust Him to "hold you up" again.

_____

_____

_____

_____

_____

_____

To access bonus materials & chapter resources, please go to

http://www.amateurnester.com/31DaysResources

And my God will meet all your needs
according to the riches of his glory in Christ Jesus.

—Philippians 4:19

I've lost all shame since becoming an infertility blogger. Want me to talk about my ovaries or my cervical mucous? No problem! Take a picture of the bruises on my stomach from IVF injections? Not a big deal!

But talk about money? I'm not so sure about that...

It's easy to complain about how expensive infertility is and how terrible insurance companies are. It's harder to talk about trusting God to provide financially.

One reason I'm so hesitant to talk about it is because I know there are many of you who haven't been able to afford treatment or testing. I don't want readers to look at my story and think, "It's easy for her to talk about God's financial provision when she's been able to afford multiple rounds of IVF. What about those of us who don't have the money?"

Quite honestly—I don't know how to answer that.

But I do know that if I believe the Bible to be true, then I have to believe what Philippians 4:19 says above. "God will meet all your needs."

So, if I can't pay for treatment does that mean God doesn't want me to pursue it?

Again, I honestly don't know.

But I do know that He promises to give us what we need in order for His planned to be fulfilled in our lives.

Maybe that's a loan with a low-interest rate.

Maybe it's financial help from friends or family.

Maybe it's a second job or insight on how to budget and save.

Perhaps it's creative ideas for fundraising.

Perhaps it's a low-cost adoption or participation in a clinical study for reduced medicine rates.

Whatever His plans are, we must trust that He will give us what we need — when we need it. Are you willing to trust that He knows what we need?

As you pray today, ask God to help you trust Him to supply the finances necessary to fulfill His plan for you. Also, consider asking Him for guidance on how to wisely manage the money you do have.

For further reflection...

How have you seen God meet your material and financial needs in the past?

_____

_____

Why is it so difficult to trust Him for finances when it comes to infertility?

_____

_____

Are you wisely managing the money you do have? What are some specific steps you can take to improve your budgeting or saving?

_____

_____

Look up the verses below. Consider writing each one out.

Proverbs 21:5, 21:20, 27:23

_____

_____

Matthew 6:31-32, 7:11

_____

_____

Write out a prayer asking God to provide for your financial needs during infertility. Commit to trusting His plans and His timing.

_____

_____

_____

_____

_____

_____

To access bonus materials & chapter resources, please go to

http://www.amateurnester.com/31DaysResources

And we know that God causes everything to work together for the good of those who love God and are called according to his purpose for them.

—Romans 8:28

Do you really believe that your infertility will be used for your good? Do you believe that He uses everything—including the tragedies, the atrocities, and the sorrows—for the good of His people? I believe it in my head, but when I turn on the news or make yet another visit to the specialist, I often have trouble believing it in my heart.

If I really believed that what Satan means for evil, God will use for my good, my life would probably look a lot different. I'd be so secure in God's promise that the anxieties, fears, and doubts I struggle with would never threaten to unhinge me. I would rest securely and peacefully in God's plan and sovereignty.

If we really believed this one promise, all the other things we're praying for during these 31 days would come a lot easier, wouldn't they?

I'm praying that God would allow this promise to sink deep down into our souls. That we would believe it with our hearts, heads, and every ounce of our beings. Will you pray that today with me, too?

For further reflection...

How would true belief in Romans 8:28 affect your daily actions and attitudes?

_____

_____

For what circumstance do you need assurance that it will work out for your good?

_____

_____

Look up the verses below. Consider writing out each one.

Genesis 50:20

_____

_____

Romans 8:35-39

_____

_____

2 Corinthians 4:15-17

_____

_____

1 Thessalonians 5:18

_____

_____

Write out a prayer below thanking God for His promise to make that circum-stance work for your good.

_____

_____

_____

_____

_____

_____

To access bonus materials & chapter resources, please go to

http://www.amateurnester.com/31DaysResources

Commit everything you do to the Lord;
trust Him and He will help you.

—Psalm 37:5

There are so many people you have to trust when you're trying to build your family.

Your doctors.

Your therapist.

Your adoption agency.

Your social worker.

Your financial adviser.

It's so important to feel like you can trust these people because they play such huge roles in helping you become a parent.

We trust these people so much that we're willing to put our bodies, our lives, and our hearts on the lines by working with them. **If we can give so much trust to imperfect human beings, why is it often so hard to trust God?**

Here is a list of what God promises us when we trust Him:

- He will help us (Psalm 37:5)

- He is our refuge (Psalm 62:8)

- He will keep us safe (Proverbs 29:25)

- He will be our shield (Proverbs 30:5)

- We will never be disgraced (Romans 10:10-12)

- Jesus will make His home in our hearts (Ephesians 3:17)

- We will share in everything that belongs to Christ (Hebrews 3:13-14)

- The salvation of our souls (1 Peter 1:9)

These promises don't mean that we'll be spared difficult times. But we can trust that even in the storms, God's love will carry us through.

As you pray today, ask God to help you put your trust in Him.

For further reflection...

Read the following quote from Charles Swindoll:

> *"We must cease striving and trust God to provide what He thinks is best and in whatever time He chooses to make it available. But this kind of trusting doesn't come naturally. It's a spiritual crisis of the will in which we must choose to exercise faith."*

Circle the phrase *we must choose*. This quote suggests that trust is not a feeling; it's a deliberate action. Do you agree?

_____

_____

It's hard to trust someone without knowing them. The more we know God, the easier it is to choose to trust Him. How can you get to know God better?

_____

_____

Look up the verses below. Consider writing out each one.

Psalm 31:14-15, 118:8

_____

_____

Isaiah 2:22, 26:4

_____

_____

John 12:44-45, 14:1

_____

_____

Romans 15:13

_____

_____

Hebrews 10:35

_____

_____

Write out a prayer below in which you commit to choose trust.

_____

_____

_____

_____

_____

_____

To access bonus materials & chapter resources, please go to

http://www.amateurnester.com/31DaysResources

For the Lord grants wisdom;
from His mouth come knowledge and understanding!

—Proverbs 2:6

I'm a reader, a researcher. I've been a knowledge geek from a very young age. In fact, I recently found a tape recording of my 7-year-old self reading aloud from an encyclopedia-like book called "How To Do Just About Anything."

So when my husband and I started trying to conceive, it was second nature for me to read as many books about pregnancy and conception I could get my hands on. My appetite for reading and researching only increased when we started seeing our infertility specialist. After each failed cycle, I'd search medical journals in hopes of figuring out which treatment or medication was right for us.

One night, after quoting some statistic I'd read, my husband gently said, "Don't you think we should spend more time asking the Lord for wisdom than searching for it online?"

His words hit me like a punch to the ovaries! I knew he was right.

It's so easy to get caught up in trying to gain wisdom on our own. But Proverbs 2:6 says that God is the One who gives wisdom, knowledge, and understanding.

Hear me out: I'm not saying we shouldn't do our homework and educate ourselves on our diagnoses and our treatment options. God also gave us brains and the capacity to learn and think. We should use those gifts to their greatest extent.

But we cannot rely on our own brains to help us fully understand or make decisions about our infertility. We must rely on God to give us the insight we need.

As you pray today, ask God to give you wisdom when making decisions about your family-building options and treatment options. Ask Him to help you rely on the knowledge He gives you—not your own understanding.

For further reflection...

What do you need wisdom for right now?

_____

_____

Jot down some thoughts on how you can fully use the gift of intellect that God has given you without becoming reliant on your own understanding.

_____

_____

Look up the verses below. Consider writing out each one.

Job 28:16-18

_____

_____

Psalm 111:10

_____

_____

The entire book of Proverbs is known as a "Wisdom Book." Check out Proverbs 19:8, 24:14, and 28:26 to start.

- Romans 11:33

- 1 Corinthians 3:19

- Colossians 2:3

Write out a prayer asking God to give you wisdom and to keep you from relying on your own understanding during your infertility journey.

_____

_____

_____

_____

_____

_____

To access bonus materials & chapter resources, please go to

http://www.amateurnester.com/31DaysResources

Enthusiasm without knowledge is no good; haste makes mistakes.

—Proverbs 19:2

Have you ever done something without really thinking it through? I recently did something that was well-intentioned, but not really thought-through. I won't go into details, but I acted quickly and foolishly, and ended up causing a scene that publicly embarrassed myself and my husband.

Perhaps the situation would've been different had I read Proverbs 19:2 before I acted hastily.

When you're walking down the road of infertility, it can feel like you're moving at an impossibly slow pace. Time is of the essence, especially if you're past a certain age. There's so much waiting. You just want to get to the next treatment or the next cycle.

But Scripture warns us not to be too hasty. We are to seek knowledge, not quick action. In our (good) desire to become parents, we need to take the time to think through our actions and our plans. How will our treatment decisions affect others? Are we making wise choices with our time and our money in our quest for parenthood? Are we honoring God with the decisions we make during this time?

These are tough questions that don't always have clear answers. But that's exactly why it's so important to take the time to pray through them and give good thought to our actions.

As you pray today, ask God to help you avoid the temptation make hasty decisions. Ask Him to give you the knowledge you need to make wise choices regarding your infertility.

For further reflection...

Read the following verses and notice their theme. What's one way to guard against making hasty decisions?

Proverbs 11:14, 12:15, 15:22, and 19:20

_____

_____

List some people you can trust to give you wise counsel.

_____

_____

Read the verses below. Consider writing out each one.

Proverbs 4:26

_____

_____

Proverbs 14: 15

_____

_____

Proverbs 21:8

_____

_____

Write out a prayer below asking God to help you guard against making hasty decisions. Ask him for people who can give you wise counsel.

_____

_____

_____

_____

_____

_____

To access bonus materials & chapter resources, please go to

http://www.amateurnester.com/31DaysResources

Above all, clothe yourselves with love,
which binds us all together in perfect harmony.

—Colossians 3:14

A recent study[1] says that couples who are unable to conceive after years of trying are three times as more likely to divorce as couples who eventually have a child.

Another study[2] says that women who are undergoing infertility treatments have a higher risk for sexual dysfunction.

And no one who has actually been through infertility would need a study to tell them about the tremendous psychological toll it takes, but there are several which concluded just that.

Higher divorce rates, sexual dysfunction, and psychological trauma... **You're naive if you think infertility won't change your marriage.**

But it doesn't have to destroy it.

I've interviewed dozens of people who've experienced infertility, and one thing they've said over and over again is that infertility, as difficult as it's been, has brought them closer with their spouse.

Of course, this "silver lining" doesn't happen accidentally or easily. It takes an intentional, deliberate choice to fight for your marriage FIRST. You must decide that your marriage is more important than your fertility, and that you're

---

1 Hillin, Taryn. "Study Reveals The Impact Failed Fertility Treatments Have On Relationships." The Huffington Post. 30 Jan. 2014. Web. 23 Oct. 2015.
2 Millheiser, Leah S., M.D., Amy E. Helmer, M.D., and Rodolfo B. Quintero, M.D. "Is Infertility a Risk Factor for Female Sexual Dysfunction? A Case-control Study." Fertility and Stertility 94.6 (2010): 2022-025. Fertility and Stertility. Web. 23 Oct. 2015.

willing to fight for it just as hard, or maybe even harder, than you fight for parenthood.

The first year of our infertility journey was the hardest on my marriage. I dealt with the bad news and frustration much differently than my husband did. It upset him that I cried so much, and it upset me that he never cried.

We both began to see how infertility could tear a marriage apart. We saw therapists separately and together. We made a decision that we wanted to be married to each other more than we wanted children. We each made sacrifices and compromises. We prayed for our marriage. We forgave each other a lot.

I realize that some of you may be in marriages where one partner refuses to talk about it or see a therapist. Or perhaps you can't afford it. **But no matter what your spouse refuses to do, you can pray.**

As you pray today, ask God to use your circumstances to bring you closer to your spouse. Also, pray for those couples whose marriages are being torn apart and ask God to bring about healing in their relationship.

For further reflection...

How has infertility affected your marriage?

_____

_____

Write down three specific ways you can show your spouse your love him or her.

1. _____

2. _____

3. _____

What area of your marriage do you need to pray for the most right now?

Read the verses below. Consider writing each one out.

Mark 10:9

_____

_____

Ephesians 4:1-2, 32

_____

_____

Colossians 4:6

_____

_____

1 Peter 4:8

_____

_____

Write out a prayer asking God to strengthen your marriage during your season of infertility.

_____

_____

_____

_____

_____

To access bonus materials & chapter resources, please go to

http://www.amateurnester.com/31DaysResources

DAY 31: PRAY FOR YOUR SPECIFIC SITUATION

Devote yourselves to prayer with
an alert mind and a thankful heart.

—Colossians 4:2

For the last thirty days you've been praying for topics I've suggested. I think they're all very worthwhile things to be praying for, but prayer is personal. We don't always need suggestions or prompts. We can come to God and pray for whatever is on our mind.

So today, let me encourage you to pray for whatever is on your heart. This is a short devotion, so use the extra few minutes to have an extended time with God.

Maybe you need to talk to Him about your specific fertility situation.

Maybe you want to go back and revisit one of our earlier topics that really spoke to you.

Or perhaps you just need to sit and listen for God's voice.

As you pray today, ask God to reveal what you two need to talk about.

For further reflection...

Is there something specific on your heart for which you need to pray today? Or, do you need to just sit and listen for God to speak?

_____

_____

_____

Read the verses below. Consider writing out each one.

Jeremiah 29:12, 33:3

_____

_____

Matthew 7:11

_____

_____

Romans 8:26

_____

_____

1 Thessalonians 5:17

_____

_____

Write out your prayer below. Or, before you sit and listen for God's voice, write a brief prayer asking Him to speak to you.

_____

_____

_____

_____

_____

_____

To access bonus materials & chapter resources, please go to

http://www.amateurnester.com/31DaysResources

ABOUT THE AUTHOR

Lisa Newton lives with her husband, Tom, on the Central California Coast. They have a daughter, C.J., who was born after multiple rounds of IVF. They also have a spoiled orange and white cat named Hemingway. In addition to maintaining AmateurNester.com, Lisa is a school library consultant for public and private school districts.

31 Days of Infertility

Day 1	Pray For Clarity	Isaiah 30:21
Day 2	Pray For Comfort	Isaiah 51:3
Day 3	Pray For Community	Galations 6:2
Day 4	Pray For Confidence	Jeremiah 17:7
Day 5	Pray For Contentment	1 Timothy 6:8
Day 6	Pray For Courage	Psalm 31:24
Day 7	Pray For Discernment	1 John 4:1
Day 8	Pray For Endurance	Colossians 1:11
Day 9	Pray For Faith	Luke 17:5
Day 10	Pray For Freedom From Fear	Psalm 34:4
Day 11	Pray For Freedom From Jealousy And Envy	Job 5:2
Day 12	Pray For Your Future Children	Isaiah 44:3
Day 13	Pray For God's Glory	Matthew 5:16
Day 14	Pray For Grace	Ephesians 6:24
Day 15	Pray For Gratefulness	1 Thessalonians 5:16-18
Day 16	Pray For Hope	Psalm 62:5
Day 17	Pray For Integrity	Proverbs 20:7
Day 18	Pray For Joy	Nehemiah 8:10
Day 19	Pray For Mercy	Psalm 28:2
Day 20	Pray To Obey	Psalm 51:12
Day 21	Pray For Others	James 5:16
Day 22	Pray For Patience	Habakkuk 2:3
Day 23	Pray For Peace	Philippians 4:7
Day 24	Pray For Strength	Psalm 73:27
Day 25	Pray For Sufficient Financeproverbs S	Philippians 4:19
Day 26	Pray For True Belief In God's Promises	Romans 8:28
Day 27	Pray For Trust	Psalm 37:5
Day 28	Pray For Wisdom	Proverbs 2:3
Day 29	Pray For Wise Decisions	Proverbs 19:2
Day 30	Pray For Your Marriage	Colossians 3:14
Day 31	Pray For Your Specific Situation	Colossians 4:2

Made in the USA
Las Vegas, NV
18 November 2023